Stop "Falling Short"

5 simple tools to banish negative perfectionism and reclaim your joy

Johanna McWeeney

Kintsugi Books

Contents

Acknowledgements	v
The Beginning	ix
1. Perfection Doesn't Exist...	1
2. The 7 Perfectionist Traps	7
3. 5 Tools to Peel Back Perfectionism and Rediscover Your Joy	23
The End	37
Further reading	39
Resources	41
About the Author	43

Stop "Falling Short" is a work of nonfiction. Some names and identifying details have been changed.

Copyright © 2023 by Johanna McWeeney. All rights reserved. No part of this book may be reproduced by any mechanical, photographic, or electronic process, other than for "fair use" as brief quotations embodied in articles and reviews, without prior written permission of the publisher.

This book is intended for educational purposes only and does not constitute medical advice. The information given in this book should not be treated as a substitute for the advice of a qualified medical professional who should always be consulted before beginning any health programme. Any use of the information in this book is at the reader's discretion and risk. The author assumes no responsibility for any adverse effects arising from the application or use of the information.

ISBN 978-1-7392581-0-8

stopfallingshort.com

Acknowledgements

I want to thank book coach extraordinaire, Vicky Quinn Fraser, for her patient encouragement, and for rekindling my love of writing. My friends Jessy and Chay for patiently reading through the first draft and telling me it didn't suck. Patrick McKeown for teaching me so much about the breath. My breathing clients, for trusting me. And you, for choosing to give your time to read this book. I hope you get something valuable from it, and that it makes a positive difference in your life.

"Perfection is just fear in high heels and a mink coat, pretending to be fancy."
Elizabeth Gilbert

The Beginning

My path to imperfection

The most enjoyable creative period in my life began with a conscious decision to stop taking any notice of other people's opinions. Not in the sense of ignoring feedback or becoming selfish. But by deliberately turning down the volume on external judgements (or my perception of them) so I could hear the small voice of my own intuition. A voice that had long been smothered by my intense self-criticism.

I've played violin since I was five years old. But from the age of 12, I was plagued with the most awful performance anxiety. It was so acute, the word "terror" would be more accurate. It first hit during a folk fiddle competition which I'd won two years in a row. This was my third shot at the trophy. I stepped up onto the stage, violin in hand, and was suddenly struck with the most appalling nerves. I'd never experienced this before, so I had no idea what was going on.

Ironically, I still played well enough to win. But my memory of that moment has none of the positive glow of success. It's full of shame for having failed. For having cracked under the pressure of my own expectations. For having let myself down in front of a crowd of onlookers.

In the months and years that followed, I became so frightened of my own fear, I took anti-anxiety medication, to stop it happening again. It still happened.

I went on to study music and work as a professional violinist but my practice was always dogged by negative perfectionism. I struggled to uncover the music, the communication, the voice inside. It felt drowned out by the lessons and suggestions of my teachers.

Somewhere along the way, in my efforts to play the perfect phrase, I'd lost any ability to express myself. Worse, in the fight to please everyone around me, to show up perfectly, I'd lost a clear sense of who I even was.

Sometimes we need a clean slate to see something that's been staring us in the face for years. I remember studying journalism and finding it easy to improve because I was less emotionally attached to the work. But it wasn't until I picked up a paintbrush for the first time in years that I found an unexpected path to freedom. Somewhere, from deep in my subconscious, came a firm decision that no matter how terrible my paintings were, I wasn't going to mind what people thought. I wasn't going to give up because they weren't good enough. I wouldn't get carried away if others told me I was talented. I was going to keep my relationship with my art sacred, and under no circumstances use it to seek approval, validation or "perfection".

This initial decision not to care what others thought became the bedrock of my progress. No longer hampered by trying to prove myself, I could handle rejection. I was able to joyfully accept my success when my work was shown at the Summer Exhibition at London's Royal Academy of Art. I was able to get myself out of the way and produce paintings that really expressed something only I could say. Because I wasn't trying to be perfect, I found an intense joy in the work, and that joy began to ripple out into my music, my writing, and my life.

Another piece of the puzzle fell into place when my work as a writer took me deep into research about the breath. I learned how stage fright, anxiety and other perfectionist symptoms show up in the body. And I learned how to restore balance, so I was less at their mercy.

I took an advanced certification in breathwork coaching and began to teach other people simple breathing exercises that unlocked their potential. Along the way, I've noticed the inner voice of perfectionism fade for my breathing clients too.

And so, I got curious. I began to read about the roots of perfectionism, and the way it manifests in systems throughout the body. And why, as I'd changed my breathing, my outlook and my creativity had become freer.

Do I still experience self doubt, mess up, and have periods of creative drought? Of course I do. But I have tools to get me back on track. I guess it's no coincidence that the word "inspiration" applies both to creativity and to the breath...

What's this book about?

This is a tiny handbook to becoming a work in progress.

In this little book, I'll share some of my experiences of perfectionism. I'll offer my understanding of where it gets lodged in the body. And I'll give you five simple tools that

The Beginning

have worked for me and others. Tools you can use to shift your perspective and move forward with more joy.

Do you need to downgrade your aspirations? No. But there is a way to let go and leave space for something better.

Something happier, more joyful, and even a little bit more... perfect.

Chapter 1

Perfection Doesn't Exist...

"I'm a perfectionist!"

There's a weight of defensive pride in that statement. It's easy to wear it as a badge of honour. In its positive form, perfectionism implies you're hard working, resourceful and driven. High standards are essential in our competitive world. And so, we think of perfectionism as the path to excellence.

But is it?

In my experience, perfectionism is often the reason we never start, or never finish our creative projects. It's an excuse for self-sabotage. It's a socially acceptable form of self-harm that crushes our creative spirit and leaves us under-achieving. It drains the joy from everything we do.

Here's the thing. Perfection doesn't exist.

"Yeah, yeah," says the perfectionist. "That might be true for you, but I'm pretty good at doing things perfectly. I'm different and special. Just you wait."

Don't listen to that voice. It's not telling the truth. The very idea of perfection is so subjective it is, by its nature, a flawed construct. Besides which, if we accept the fact that most of us learn our best lessons by making mistakes, we have to acknowledge that striving to be perfect straight off the blocks denies us the opportunity to grow. Thomas Edison, for example, invented 10,000 lightbulbs that didn't work before he created one that did. If he'd allowed perfectionism to get in his way, you might still be reading this by candlelight.

I read an allegorical story recently of a man who wanted to walk a particular path, but a large boulder blocked his way. He chipped away at the boulder for days, trying to break it so he could continue his journey. Eventually, after much effort, he split the rock in two. Immediately, the sun shone between the two great lumps of stone, hewn apart by his tremendous effort, and he was bathed in light. Suddenly, the path forward was clear. The story went on to explain that the boulder represented the negative thought patterns we place in our own way. Essentially, the man had placed the barrier in his own path, blocking his own light.

Maybe it helps to think of perfectionism as a giant rock. It certainly stops us moving forward, and it blocks our light. You can't get over it, or round it, because it fills your field of vision. The crazy thing is, it's an obstacle you've placed in your own way, through years of conditioning and confusion.

And yes, knowing this is one thing. Accepting it is another. And then, what are you supposed to do about it? The common advice to let go of limiting beliefs is unhelpful and demoralising, and there's a reason why it doesn't work. We'll get into that later, but first, let's take an objective look at perfectionism and how it affects our ability to express and enjoy ourselves.

The dark side of perfectionism

Research identifies two distinct types of perfectionism. There's adaptive perfectionism, also called positive striving. This involves putting significant effort towards achieving your goals. It's about having high standards and working hard to meet them[1].

Then there's maladaptive perfectionism – the evil twin. With this negative manifestation, we're more concerned with the way others see us. Our inner voice is heavily self-critical. Psychologists define this type of perfectionism as a combination of impossibly high standards with an overly critical inner voice. Perfectionists ascribe an *irrational* importance to being perfect. We are punitive in our self-evaluation and our self esteem is fragile.

We believe the inner voice

What's more, this inner criticism actually stops us from being able to achieve what we want.

Research from NASA scientists reveals that 98% of four and five-year-olds operate at a "genius" level creatively. Genius happens when we're able to absorb and synthesise information from our senses, intuition, intellect and perception.

By the time we're adults, only 2% of us still have the capacity for creative genius. Over the years, we disconnect from our natural abilities. We look outside ourselves for approval. And this learned voice of inner judgement – the voice that is so loud in the perfectionist mind – makes us wrong. Our belief about what is and isn't possible becomes condition based. And so, we strive for perfection against the odds. Against an inner belief that we are somehow flawed.

I believe negative self-talk is a coping mechanism. If we can catch our mistakes before anyone else sees them, we will protect ourselves from the shame and embarrassment of having them pointed out. If we self-sabotage, we don't need to fear failure, because we can predict it. We can protect ourselves from disappointment by ensuring we never expect anything.

The result is that we keep ourselves small. We blame situations, circumstances, and other people for our lack of progress. Deep down, we believe we're not good enough. And we set out to prove it to ourselves, over and over again.

In our desire to be perfect, we limit our ability to succeed.

The spiralling cost of perfectionism

At its most damaging, negative perfectionism – falling short of the ideal self – can contribute to eating disorders[2]. It makes you more vulnerable to depression[3]. And it's associated with addiction to exercise[4], internet use[5], and substances including drugs and alcohol[6].

What's more, it has a direct negative impact on our ability to enjoy life. It leads to burnout, anxiety, and sleep disorders. It makes you more vulnerable to physical pain. And it may even shorten your life.

Sounds dramatic?

The stress caused by continually trying to achieve the impossible contributes to physical and mental disease. Long-running research shows that in the US, Canada and the UK, perfectionism has increased in the last three decades[7]. The researchers draw the stark conclusion that the rise in socially prescribed perfectionism – perfectionism motivated by the need to gain approval from others – may explain the rise in mental health problems among young people[8]. In other words, it's no coincidence we have reached a point at which stress is the number one cause of illness in Western society.

Where there is stress, there is dis-ease. And without ease, joy cannot thrive.

---

1. Haynos, Ann F., et al. "Subtypes of adaptive and maladaptive perfectionism in anorexia nervosa: Associations with eating disorder and affective symptoms." Journal of Psychopathology and Behavioral Assessment 40.4 (2018): 691-700.
2. Haynos, Ann F., et al. "Subtypes of adaptive and maladaptive perfectionism in anorexia nervosa: Associations with eating disorder and affective symptoms." Journal of Psychopathology and Behavioral Assessment 40.4 (2018): 691-700.
3. Nealis, Logan J., et al. "Self-critical perfectionism, depressive symptoms, and HPA-axis dysregulation: Testing emotional and physiological stress reactivity." Journal of Psychopathology and Behavioral Assessment 42.3 (2020): 570-581.
4. Çakın, Gizem, et al. "Exercise addiction and perfectionism: a systematic review of the literature." Current Addiction Reports 8.1 (2021): 144-155.
5. Yang, Wenjie, et al. "Maladaptive perfectionism and internet addiction among Chinese college students: a moderated mediation model of depression and gender." International journal of environmental research and public health 18.5 (2021): 2748.
6. Canning, Jessica R., et al. "Perfectionism discrepancy and falling short of the ideal self: Investigating drinking motives and impaired control on the road to alcohol-related problems." Personality and individual differences 159 (2020): 109909.
7. Curran, Thomas, and Andrew P. Hill. "Perfectionism is increasing over time: A meta-analysis of birth cohort differences from 1989 to 2016." Psychological bulletin 145.4 (2019): 410.
8. Curran, Thomas, and Andrew P. Hill. "Perfectionism is increasing over time: A meta-analysis of birth cohort differences from 1989 to 2016." Psychological bulletin 145.4 (2019): 410.

Chapter 2

The 7 Perfectionist Traps

If you're reading this book, chances are, you're aware you have some issues with perfectionism. But perfectionism is a sneaky animal. It doesn't always look like you might expect. My own perfectionism shows up in many ways. It's a shape-shifter. A chameleon. It pretends to be something else. Sometimes it manifests as anxiety or depression. But just as often, it shows up in my behaviours and attitudes.

You might recognise yourself in some of these seven perfectionist traps...

Trap #1: You experience imposter syndrome

If you always have to be perfect, you're never going to be good enough. You'll take this fear of failure into every project. Creative work is impossible unless you can approach it with an explorative mind. What's more, imposter syndrome is not so much about feeling out of your depth; it's fear of being found out. And if you take every step under the weight of perceived criticism and opinions from others, you're carrying a heavy load. You'll inevitably feel like you're falling short.

The sense of being a fake is part of the creative process, because creativity comes from somewhere deeper than our intelligence. It happens through us, not in us. I take heart from the fact that Leonard Cohen, one of the most virtuosic and prolific songwriters and poets to have lived, wrote in his poem, *Thousands*, "I am one of the fakes."

Trap #2: You've suffered with "stage fright" that negatively affects your performance

My first study, and first profession, was classical music. I love music. And ever since I was four years old, I knew I wanted to be a violinist. But from the age of 12, I was crippled by performance anxiety. I would try to resolve it by practising harder – an approach that looked very much like adaptive perfectionism. Except my focus wasn't on creating. I was busy trying to play how others thought I should. I'd approach every performance believing that, if only I could be perfect, there'd be nothing to feel anxious about. I desperately wanted the feelings to go away. Very quickly, I became anxious about the anxiety itself – a negative spiral that took all the joy from the work.

Trap #3: Your self talk is borderline abusive

"You idiot," I blurted, angrily. I was standing in my kitchen alone. Talking to myself.

I had cooked some sausages. And just after I'd taken them out of the oven, I picked up the hot tray with my bare hands. For a moment, jolted back to reality by the sound of my own voice, I saw it. Just how unkind I am to myself. I made myself stop. I apologised to myself, out loud, just as I'd cursed myself out loud. It made me think. If I'm that hard on myself over something so small, imagine how horrible I am with things that really matter.

I think a lot, so I went deeper with this idea. I like to imagine I wouldn't speak to another person so unkindly. But the truth is, when it's so habitual in my inner dialogue, it does sometimes come out in my interactions with others. It also means I've allowed others to speak to me in a totally unacceptable way.

How do you speak to yourself when you make a mistake?

I tend to default to calling myself stupid. Because, as a perfectionist, being stupid is the worst possible crime. Just being aware of this shines a light on it. It puts it in perspective. Picking up the sausages with bare hands does not render my entire contribution to humanity worthless, even if it temporarily removes my fingerprints.

Trap #4: You have unreasonable expectations of others

If your expectations of yourself are impossibly high, and you're constantly looking over your shoulder to gauge people's opinions, you may notice you're unintentionally hard on others. This can make it difficult to feel liked. When negative self-talk leaks out into our interactions with friends, family, and co-workers, they're likely to react badly.

I used to get constantly stressed with people for not doing things the way I thought they should be done. Underneath that stress, control, and at times, borderline dictatorship, was my own fear that I was going to mess up. Or that if the whole thing fell apart, I would be held accountable.

Trap #5: You find it almost impossible to say "no"

When part of you believes that you have to be perfect to be acceptable, you'll start to say "yes" to everything you're asked to do. This goes beyond people-pleasing. It's an inner need to be indispensable. To be valued for your contribution.

Here's the thing: it doesn't work. If you never say no, rather than feeling valued, you'll start to feel that people are taking advantage.

For years, I would agree to do things for my writing clients that I didn't know how to do. I'd say "yes," then find out. I'd learn unfamiliar software, and go miles outside my skill set, because I thought I had to. Not only was I wasting my time on things I wasn't particularly good at, I was spending hours doing tasks I didn't even *want* to do. I'd feel miserable, and I had nobody to blame but myself.

Things changed for me when I started saying "no." When I stopped trying to be perfect at everything, I gave myself more time to be *good enough* at one thing. And far from complaining, clients even welcomed it. One business owner, when I said a firm "no" to doing something outside of the writing work we'd agreed, replied, "I appreciate you leaning into the zone of your genius." Well, how about that?!

Trap #6: You never finish a project

An unfinished project still has the potential to be perfect.

For a while, I lived with someone who had this pattern of perfectionism. The entire house was a mess of incomplete DIY projects. None of the rooms had a single paint colour. You only had to move a piece of furniture to find one of the previous decorative iterations. Tiles were missing from the floor. It was chaos. If you regularly start things only for them to languish in various stages of incompletion, perfectionism may be to blame.

Trap #7: You never START a project (procrastination)

Even when something is good for you, and you want to do it, you can't seem to get started. Something is holding you back. It's normally fear.

We're told all the time that to do something well, we must be willing to do it badly. It always struck me that telling this to a perfectionist was rather like asking a fish to climb a tree. Luckily, I believe it's simpler and less painful than that. To do something well enough, we must be willing to *start*. And to start without fixating on a specific outcome.

There's a reason why affirmations and visualisation techniques often finish with the request, "This or something better." It's that we can rarely, if ever, see the bigger picture. By letting go of outcomes, it's entirely possible we'll achieve something far greater than we first imagined.

At the same time, a good or "perfect" outcome is subjective. If you look back over your life, you'll see many examples of outcomes you strived for. You'll see that, when you seemingly fell short, life had other plans for you that had their own rewards. Some of the greatest moments in my life would never have happened if I hadn't previously "failed" and been redirected.

For me, this trap manifests in weird ways. I may delay trying on clothes I ordered online. My fear is that they won't fit, and I'll have a minor crisis about my body image. Or I may put off starting an important writing job because I can't yet see how the finished piece will look. Trying to imagine perfection, I become quickly overwhelmed at the apparent scope of the job. I have to remind myself to keep things simple and just start.

In this trap, it can be helpful to ask yourself, "What's the worst possible outcome?" It sounds fatalistic, but sometimes, when we identify the most catastrophic result from our efforts, we can see that it's pretty unlikely to happen. And we can begin to recognise that, in most cases, it's not even that scary. If the worst happens, we can probably handle it.

In his beautiful book on Celtic spirituality, *Anam Cara*, John O'Donohue explains that identifying the thing we're afraid of is a liberating process: "Fear is like fog; it spreads everywhere and falsifies the shape of everything," he says. "When you pin it down to that one question, it shrinks back to a proportion that you are able to engage. When you can name your fear, your fear begins to shrink."

Which takes me to the big question I ask when I find myself in one of these perfectionist traps. **What am I afraid of?**

What *are* you afraid of?

At its core, negative perfectionism is a coping mechanism designed to protect us from fear. Fear of what? Mostly fear of being rejected by others. One of my biggest fears has always been that **there's something wrong with me**, and that one day, people will find out. What would happen if they did? I'd be rejected. I play this out in many ways, and one of those is perfectionism.

Another common fear, similar but distinct from the example above, is that **we aren't good enough**. Good enough for what? When we externalise our standards, we're never good enough to be accepted by others. We fear that one day they'll find out, and we'll be rejected.

Deep down, we all need to fit in. To be accepted by others. On a biological level, it's vital for humans to connect with each other to survive as a species. For our distant ancestors, rejection would mean certain death. The brain still prioritises these biological needs. And it's very attracted to fear. Fear lives in the nervous system as an evolutionary response that is designed to keep us alive.

The brain sees it this way: if we fail, we might die.

Identifying your fear

Take a moment to think about something that's worrying you right now. Perhaps it's a task you haven't started yet. Or something you planned to do, but never finished. Maybe there's something you're dreading – a performance or a presentation, for instance. You've put the work in, but somehow you still feel worried about the results. Or is there a conversation you're avoiding or an email you just can't hit "send" on? Stop for a moment. Can you imagine stepping outside of your body? Standing a little behind yourself and observing the situation from a distance?

What are you afraid of? What's under that fear? And that one? What's the worst possible outcome? What are you *really* afraid of? Here's an example... For some reason, I can't make myself send an email quoting a client for a job. I've cleaned the bathroom, been for a walk, given my houseplant a haircut... But the email is still sitting in drafts.

What am I afraid of?

Johanna McWeeney

I'm afraid the client will think the quote is too high

↓

I'm afraid they'll ask, "Who does she think she is?" (ridicule/rejection)

↓

I'm afraid I won't have the skill to deliver (imposter syndrome)

↓

I'm afraid I'll fail

↓

I'm afraid everyone will know there's something wrong with me

↓

I'm afraid of the shame

↓

I'm afraid I'll be rejected

↓

I'm afraid I'll die

When I map it out like this, it's much easier to see that the underlying fear is illogical. I can view the situation in the light of my previous experience. Have any of these outcomes happened before? Have I died?

By naming my fear, I can right-size it. And then I can ask a better question.

What small step can I take to move things forward?

In this case, the answer is simple. Send the damn email and see what happens. The worst possible outcome is that I never get a reply. And I know from experience, that just means this opportunity wasn't the right fit. So either way, it's a win.

Why does fear steal joy?

The body is primed to respond to threat via the autonomic nervous system. This system is responsible for regulating the body's automatic functions. Unconscious processes like the beating of the heart, the rise and fall of blood pressure, and the life-giving process of breathing.

The autonomic nervous system has two balancing branches. The sympathetic nervous system, which you'll know as your "fight, flight or freeze" response. And the parasympathetic nervous system, which is often called the "rest and digest" response.

The sympathetic nervous system activates in response to fear. When this happens, the body reacts. So does the brain. Any functions that won't help you fight or flee simply shut down. This includes the intelligent, reasoning parts of your brain that help you make good decisions. Over time, a heightened stress response causes brain cells to die, making your brain smaller. This means the hypervigilance that comes from negative perfectionism could feasibly make you less able to perform well. What's more, it's possible to be in a state of fear without feeling afraid[1].

Research shows that negative perfectionism is strongly linked with sympathetic activation, stress reactivity and higher cortisol levels during even low-stress situations[2]. Conversely, adaptive perfectionism and its associated flow states require a balanced nervous system. One that's responsive to external and internal change, not reactive.

In negative perfectionism, the drive to do something perfectly is designed to keep us safe. But the state it creates in the body and mind, is not one of wellbeing. And it's not one that allows us to live creatively either.

While fear is associated with the evolutionary stress response, joy, with its feelings of freedom, safety, and ease[3], increases activity in the parasympathetic nervous system[4]. To experience joy, we need to be able to let go of stress from a physiological perspective.

If anyone has ever told you to "Calm down," you'll know how irritating and unhelpful that is. Instead, you need a tool that taps into the nervous system and turns the needle away from stress, and towards balance.

And that tool is your breath.

How can something so simple be the answer?

As I mentioned earlier, your autonomic nervous system controls the automatic functions that maintain balance in the body, sustaining life, and helping you respond to internal and external stimuli. The unique thing about the breath is that, while it carries on unconsciously most of the time, you can choose to control and change it. And when you do this, you influence the nervous system, altering your heartbeat, and changing your blood chemistry. This means you can consciously create better conditions in the body – conditions that support clearer thinking and a relaxed state of focus.

With regular practice, the nervous system becomes more responsive and flexible. You become more highly tuned, self-assured, and able to deal with daily challenges. You can regulate the fear response and become more receptive to joy.

If it's that simple, why isn't everyone practising breathing exercises? Well, as humans we tend to wait until we reach crisis point before we act. We're conditioned to treat the symptoms of dis-ease, not address the underlying causes. What's more, it's possible to become so acclimatised to a high level of stress, we may not even acknowledge we're struggling until our physical or mental health breaks down.

Another problem is that breathing is such a universal function it's easy to laugh at it. When I first mentioned to friends that I was coaching people how to breathe, there was about a 30% chance that someone would quip, "I already know how to breathe," or "Breathing? I've been doing it for years!"

The thing is, we all breathe. But lifestyle, postural habits, lack of understanding and other factors mean that most of us have unhealthy breathing habits. And guess what? They're compounding our stress and making us sick.

Another sticking point is that breathing exercises can feel uncomfortable and even boring. They're often taught incorrectly. Perhaps you've had an experience with mindfulness or meditation that was so mentally or physically uncomfortable it put you off trying any of this "woowoo" stuff ever again. Plus, it's just something else to do, and really, who has the time? Well, I'd say you're quite right. If you never look at your breathing habits, and you stay stuck in chronic stress, research suggests your life will be shorter. So you'd better get on with finishing that thing you're doing, right?

The good news is, this isn't going to take hours of your day. I've suggested five simple tools to help, and if you only ever use the first one, you will have made a significant, lifelong difference to your wellbeing. Even better, since you're breathing all the time, you can get plenty of practice while you're otherwise just carrying on with your life.

There's one more objection to breathing exercises. It's the feeling that you've tried everything, and nothing has worked. That feeling can engender a deep sense of failure. You may find yourself thinking, "This may work for other people, but it won't work for me."

Yes, it will. There's an innate link between your breath and your nervous system. This isn't some sort of toxic positivity practice. When you change the balance of your nervous system, your physiology changes, and that has a direct impact on brain function and emotions. It's not a trick, a hack, or a quick fix. It works for everyone to the extent that they use it.

And if it's taken you to be today-years-old to realise you have this power within you, that's fine. We all have our own journeys, and we have them for a reason. For instance, if I hadn't been such a slow learner, I'd never have written this book.

So, if you find yourself resistant to this idea, I want to ask you three simple questions. Answer them honestly. You aren't sharing the answers with anyone.

1. How long has negative perfectionism been a problem for you?

2. What's the benefit of staying where you are now?
3. *What's the cost* of staying where you are now?

What is the cost? Is it costing you your happiness? Then let's try something to change that.

Fright, or flight?

At the start of this book I described my struggle with stage fright. And later, I explained that stage fright is one of the perfectionist traps. But how does it connect with the breath?

Well, studies of music students have shown that the symptoms of stage fright stem from breathing too much air. How many times, when you were nervous about something, has someone told you to, "Take a big, deep breath?" Go on. Take one now...

Take a big, deep breath.

Okay. Now can you tell me, was that a slow, silent breath through your nose? Or was it a large gulp of air that never got deeper than your upper chest?

There isn't space in this book to explain the minutiae of breathing physiology, and there are other books that cover the info if you're interested. But there's some simple stuff that's worth knowing.

When you take a large breath in, you take a large, heavy breath out. This reduces levels of carbon dioxide (CO_2) in your blood. CO_2 is important for lots of reasons. Not least that it's responsible for releasing oxygen from the blood so your body can use it to make energy. It also dilates blood vessels, so blood can circulate better, carrying oxygen to every cell of your body and brain.

When you take a big, heavy breath out, CO_2 levels

drop, blood vessels constrict and oxygen can't get where it's needed. This habit of breathing an excessive volume of air so that CO_2 reduces has a name. It's called hyperventilation. And just like stress can be chronic as well as acute, it's not always characterised by panic and a brown paper bag. More often, you might experience cold hands, yawning, sighing, lightheadedness, anxiety, IBS, lower back pain, panic attacks, and dozens of other symptoms.

So, back to the freezing hands, body shakes, and terrifying sense of dissociation you feel as you stand in the wings waiting to go on stage, gazing glassy-eyed at the sign that some wag has graffitied to read "Stage (f)Right" and wishing you found it funny.

Scientists have shown that people who experience performance anxiety also demonstrate irregular breathing patterns before they perform. So I'm going to suggest something contentious.

Whatever you do, *don't* take a big, deep breath.

One of the main reasons I began to take the breath seriously was the impact it had on my ability to enjoy performing. It's hard not to change your breathing when you write about it for three years straight.

As I grew in understanding, instead of taking big breaths to calm down, I found myself reducing my breath, quieting it, breathing slowly and taking in less air. When you do this, CO_2 increases in your lungs and blood. Blood vessels dilate, circulation improves, and your fingers feel toasty warm. Gone is the feeling that you can't possibly perform with these two blocks of ice at the end of your arms.

Blood vessels open in the brain too, flooding the brain cells with oxygen. You can think more clearly. The nervous system is balanced, rather than powering forward in fight or flight mode.

This goes far deeper than changing your mindset. You're altering the physiological parameters that create the symptoms you experience as stage fright. You may still get the shakes to begin with, but it won't be so bad. And there's a distinct chance that, if you've done the work (which of course, you have) you'll enter flow state and enjoy your performance.

After the COVID lockdowns ended, I remember sitting in the opera pit in front of my first live audience in two years. I remember the warm glow in my fingers, the feeling of calm excitement, the smile on my face. I remember the music. I remember the enjoyment. And I remember thinking, "There's definitely something in all this breathing stuff."

---

1. Steimer, Thierry. "The biology of fear-and anxiety-related behaviors." Dialogues in clinical neuroscience (2022).
2. Nealis, Logan J., et al. "Self-critical perfectionism, depressive symptoms, and HPA-axis dysregulation: Testing emotional and physiological stress reactivity." Journal of Psychopathology and Behavioral Assessment 42.3 (2020): 570-581.
3. Johnson, Matthew Kuan. "Joy: A review of the literature and suggestions for future directions." The Journal of Positive Psychology 15.1 (2020): 5-24.
4. Kop, Willem J., et al. "Autonomic nervous system reactivity to positive and negative mood induction: The role of acute psychological responses and frontal electrocortical activity." Biological psychology 86.3 (2011): 230-238.

Chapter 3

5 Tools to Peel Back Perfectionism and Rediscover Your Joy

Tool #1: Change your breathing, change your story

Sandra first emailed me about breath coaching in February 2022. She was in her early fifties and struggling with her health. She'd gone from scaling Mont Blanc several times a season to finding it hard to breathe just climbing the stairs. She would find herself wheezing so much that by the time she reached the top, she couldn't speak. She'd been a professional athlete, and she was in a high-pressure, high-profile job. I figured it was likely she was a perfectionist.

I fixed a call to speak with Sandra to see if I could help. During that first call, I could already see the problem. High levels of daily stress, compounded by a few acutely challenging events, had tipped her nervous system into chronic imbalance. Positive striving had become a negative coping mechanism and her body was creating symptoms under the strain. When Sandra spoke, her breath came in loud gasps.

She wasn't sleeping well, and her breathing was perpetuating the problem.

The first thing I asked Sandra to do was to pay attention to whether she was breathing through her mouth or her nose. She was noticeably mouth breathing when she talked, but were there other times she slipped into this habit too?

Nasal breathing is the first step to a balanced nervous system. The human brain can only survive for a few minutes without oxygen, and the mouth provides an alternative breathing route if the nose is blocked. But mouth breathing is associated with disease. We humans are meant to breathe through our noses.

The nose has many useful functions. It purifies and conditions inhaled air, so it arrives in our lungs clean, warm, and humid. But nasal breathing is also vital if you want to move away from that perfectionism-activated sympathetic nervous system and develop the ability to relax and go with the flow.

When you breathe through your nose, the breathing naturally slows down. The nose creates much more resistance to airflow than the mouth. Think about it this way. When you drink through a straw, your piña colada arrives in your mouth in a slow, delicious stream, rather than a chilled gulp. When you breathe through your nose, the air enters your lungs more slowly, and it stays there for longer before you breathe it out. This helps with oxygenation. It also begins to activate the relaxation response, balancing your nervous system away from fight or flight.

What's more, nose breathing engages the diaphragm – your main breathing muscle, while mouth breathing tends to be fast, shallow and into the upper chest. Even if you know nothing about breathing, you probably know that fast, upper-chest breathing is synonymous with anxiety and fear.

There's that word "fear" again.

In the brain, mouth breathing stimulates the amygdala. The amygdala is the part of the brain where the fight or flight response begins. It signals the pituitary gland to release stress hormones into the body. Breathing becomes faster, the heart races, the gut clenches and we get trapped in a sort of tunnel vision[1].

Mouth breathing compounds feelings of fear, but nose breathing activates different neural pathways. When you breathe through your nose, areas of the brain associated with cognitive function, good decision-making and memory synchronise[2]. Stress hormones decrease, and dopamine levels increase[3]. And, because nose breathing is usually slower, it sends signals of safety back to the brain. Because this creates a different chemistry in your body, one that's less fear-driven and more balanced, this body-to-brain signal is *much* more effective than someone telling you to calm down.

Sandra and I had our second online breath coaching session a fortnight after the first. She burst into the call early, beaming from ear to ear. "The change has been PROFOUND! I know it's early days, but I feel so much better."

I'd suggested she practise a short guided meditation each night before bed, and this, alongside the nasal breathing, had been the wake-up call she needed to carry on with the breath training. "It's been so long since I slowed down and made that time for myself," she told me. "I didn't even realise I was so stressed."

But the reason I'm telling you this story is what happened next. Over the following weeks and months, I watched Sandra embrace this new way of being. She actively took time to nurture the rest and digest part of her nervous system, building its strength like a muscle. With her nervous system less reactive, she became less competitive and much nicer to herself. Her perfectionism began to rebalance itself, giving way to a sort of calm determination that looked very much like the positive striving of adaptive perfectionism. Her fitness began to improve. She was able to sail through challenging situations, and she was able to achieve more with less effort.

And guess what? She was happy!

Of course, during our months of breath coaching, we did more than just focus on nose breathing. But perfectionism is associated with a heightened stress response. And the first step to balancing your stress response is to breathe through your nose. By switching to nasal breathing, you can begin to change your inner story and rebalance your negative perfectionism.

Action step:

Begin to notice throughout your day whether you habitually breathe through your mouth. Perhaps while you're working at the computer, or when you exercise? Maybe you wake yourself up snoring at night?

Can you switch to nose breathing 24/7? Breathing expert Patrick McKeown and author James Nestor both recommend taping the mouth to sleep. If that's something you're willing to try, you just need a small piece of paper medical tape, a bit of persistence and a sense of humour.

If you're interested in finding out more about the benefits and practise of nose breathing, *Breath, the New Science of a Lost Art*, by James Nestor and *The Breathing Cure* by Patrick McKeown are both useful resources.

Tool #2: Restore balance

After you've switched to nasal breathing, the next step is to give your nervous system a bit of love. If you've been stuck in chronic stress for a while, you'll need to spend some time each day in parasympathetic dominance. By this I mean you need to do more than sit down with the intention to relax. You need a tool that activates your parasympathetic nervous system, rebalancing stress from a physiological perspective. Again, the key tool is your breath.

By working with the breath in a very specific way, it's possible to activate the vagus nerve. The vagus nerve is an important cranial nerve (meaning it starts in the brain). It regulates your parasympathetic nervous system. When the vagus nerve activates, it releases a neurotransmitter called acetylcholine, which slows your heart. This sends signals from your body to your brain, letting your systems know you are safe.

The vagus nerve activates each time we exhale. So by slowing the breath and lengthening your exhalation, you can directly tap into your nervous system and begin to restore balance.

Action step:

For this practice, I want you to forget everything you already know about slow breathing. I don't want you to breathe into your belly, breathe with any sound or try to fill your lungs to the top.

I want you to breathe softly and silently, in and out through your nose, focusing only on the feeling of air as it moves in and out of your nostrils. Allow each breath to be quite small, without forcing. You might feel as if you'd like to take a bigger breath, and that's okay.

- *Sit upright in a chair or lie on the floor*
- *Allow your spine to lengthen so the space between your ribs begins to widen*
- *Let your shoulders, neck, jaw and tummy relax*
- *Now, bring your attention to your breath*
- *Focus on the feeling of air as it flows in and out through your nose*
- *And when you're ready, begin to count*
- *Breathe in for four*
- *Breathe out for six*
- *Breathing softly in for four*
- *Allowing a soft breath out for six*
- *Breathing in for four*
- *And out for six*
- *Keep your breathing light, and allow your body to relax as you continue counting your breath in and out*

Continue this exercise for at least 5 minutes. To begin with, practise it 4 or 5 times a day, or whenever you remember.

This breathing pattern slows the breath to six breaths a minute. Countless studies have shown that this breathing pace optimises parasympathetic activation. This is a great exercise to do just before sleep. And it is helpful for clobbering fear and reducing symptoms of stage fright.

Tool #3: Find your flow

I recently heard breathwork pioneer Dan Brulé say that those people who are in the top 1% in their chosen profession are all good breathers. There's a reason for this. Adaptive perfectionism – the good kind, where we work really hard at something and get good at it – flows from a balanced state.

During adaptive performance, both branches of the nervous system are active[4]. Research shows that co-activation of the sympathetic and parasympathetic nervous systems is necessary for optimal short-term mental engagement.

This choreographed poise between systems reflects greater autonomic balance. A balanced system is flexible, and this flexibility is necessary if you want to achieve flow state – the state of oneness with your task in which you produce your best work, feel happiest and may be *nearest* to your ideal of perfection.

Action step:

To activate both branches of your nervous system, helping you find this optimal mental state, you can use a simple exercise called box breathing. This exercise is popular among elite military special forces, who use it to promote this kind of relaxed mental focus. To practise, you'll need the stopwatch on your smartphone or watch, or a timepiece with a second count.

Here's how to do the exercise:

- *Sit upright in a chair or lie on the floor*

- *Allow your spine to lengthen so the space between your ribs begins to widen*
- *Let your shoulders, neck, jaw and tummy relax*
- *Now, bring your attention to your breath*
- *Focus on the feeling of air as it flows in and out through your nose*
- *And when you're ready, begin to count*
- *Breathe in for four*
- *Hold for four*
- *Breathe out for four*
- *Hold for four*
- *Breathe in for four*
- *Hold for four*
- *Breathe out for four*
- *Hold for four*
- *Continue to breathe in this "box" shaped even pattern for around 5 minutes*

As you practise the exercise, keep your attention on the feeling of air as it enters and leaves your nose. There's no need to take big breaths in or to "fill" your lungs. Just keep counting and breathing silently and softly through your nose.

If the breathing pattern feels too slow for you, count 2 or 3 for each part of the breath instead. Just as long as the in-breath, hold, exhale and hold are all the same length.

You can repeat this exercise several times a day, whenever you want to focus your mind.

Tool #4: Sleep

I touched on this in Tool #1, but if you breathe through your mouth during the day, chances are you do at night too. You may notice that you wake up in the morning with a dry mouth and terrible morning breath. This is a good indicator that you were mouth breathing.

The same goes for other breathing habits. If your everyday breathing is fast and shallow, your breathing will be fast and shallow when you sleep. The good news is, as you address your daytime breathing, your nighttime breathing will improve too. This is incredibly important because your sleep quality affects your stress levels, your ability to perform well, and your long-term wellbeing.

The usual advice for a good night's sleep is to aim for around eight hours shut-eye, don't do screen-time or drink alcohol just before bed, don't eat too late... There's a prohibitive list of suggestions that just don't always gel with the way we want to spend the evening, watching a late-night movie with a glass of wine and a plate of cheese, before rolling into bed at midnight for a 6am start.

You'll have read this stuff a million times, and probably still don't feel like doing it, no matter how groggy you feel in the morning.

Action step:

To ensure better quality sleep, you can try three things I've already described in Tools #1 and #2. First, switch to nose breathing during the day, whatever you're doing. It will begin to retrain your body so nasal breathing becomes the new norm.

The only sure-fire way to ensure you breathe through your nose during sleep is to tape your mouth. If you don't fancy the medical paper tape, you can try one of the custom sleep tapes on the market.

If you're frightened of suffocating, there's even a tape

that doesn't cover the mouth at all. It's called MyoTape. It's available at oxygenadvantage.com, and I've included a link in the resources at the end of the book. Expect the tape to come off during the night for the first week or so, but persist with it. You may notice that you snore less, and that you wake feeling fresher in the morning.

If you struggle to breathe through your nose, try a nasal dilator for sleep. And if your nose really is blocked because of injury, polyps or suchlike, talk to your doctor.

Second, as I mentioned, practise the slow breathing exercise for ten minutes before sleep. It will help you get to sleep faster, and it may mean you wake less often during the night. When the body is less hyper-reactive because of stress, it's easier to get to sleep and stay asleep.

Important note:

Never tape your mouth if you feel nauseous, or if you've been drinking alcohol or taken anything else that's likely to affect your ability to wake up. When using specialist mouth tape, always follow the directions on the pack.

Tool #5: Permission to be human

Right near the start of this book, I mentioned that perfection doesn't exist. This isn't absolutely true. I certainly can't look at the furled petals of a June rose, or the blanket of stars in a clear night sky without feeling inspired by their perfectness.

What I really meant is that, when we humans aim for perfection, we cause ourselves pain. This constant striving comes from a place of self-doubt, and masks a feeling we are somehow inadequate – that we're not good enough just as we are.

As I was thinking about this, the phrase popped into my head, "To err is human, to forgive is divine." It made me think: I've never been able to change the way I approach any problem unless I'm willing to do it from a place of self love. In other words, if I'm full of shame or self-blame for having caused myself the problem, or stayed stuck in it so long, I'm going to find it very difficult to move forward.

Perfectionism isn't intrinsically bad. We need to strive to reach our goals. Each of us has a strong creative drive and a desire to do something with our lives. This need for fuller, freer expression of the self is present in every single living thing, and it's described beautifully in the Talmud, which says, "Every blade of grass has an angel that bends over it and whispers, 'Grow, grow.'" That said, if you're able to remember the maxim, "progress not perfection," it becomes much easier to feel that you're getting somewhere.

If your journey has been a little harder than it could've been, because you placed the big rock of perfectionism in your own path, it's important not to beat yourself up about that. To move forward, you may need to practise being kind to yourself. This can be a powerful tool, because it allows you to notice and change your habitual behaviour without judging yourself so harshly.

There's a lovely Hawaiian prayer called ho'oponopono that offers a gentle practice of self-forgiveness. It consists of a four-step mantra, which you can use as a simple meditation.

"I'm sorry, please forgive me, thank you, I love you."

Action step:

Find a quiet place to sit, and settle down comfortably. If you like, you can light a candle or burn some incense. Close your eyes, and set an intention for self forgiveness.

Set the intention to release all those moments where

negative perfectionism held you back. To forgive yourself for the harsh words you said to yourself, and to accept that you did the best you could. To allow for the possibility that you might just be good enough, exactly as you are. And be open to trying something different from now on, or at least for this one day, which is all you really have.

Allow the mantra to enter your thoughts. Focus on the words as you repeat them to yourself.

"I'm sorry, please forgive me, thank you, I love you."

Have the intention to welcome whatever feelings come up. Whatever emotions surface. You might like to sit here for a couple of minutes, or longer. Make a daily practice of this for at least three weeks. Follow it with the slow breathing exercise and notice if anything changes.

A few ideas to take it a bit further

Thank you

It may seem unrelated, but one of the most powerful things I ever did to unpick my negative perfectionism was to begin a daily gratitude list. Being a perfectionist, the only way I was able to maintain the practice was to write my list in a page-a-day diary. This had the effect of making it obvious if I skipped a day, and as a result, I never have.

How does gratitude help? Well, scientists have shown that a gratitude practice activates the vagus nerve. What's more, by finding small things to be grateful for every day, no matter how mundane or silly they feel, we rewire our brains to see more good in our lives. And when we see more good in our lives, we don't get so caught up in the feelings of inadequacy that drive negative perfectionism.

I love you

For most of us, the idea of saying, "I love you," to ourselves is uncomfortable, or at least unfamiliar. But often, the person we hurt most on our journey through life is ourselves.

For a time, I found self-love so difficult, I actually bought myself a decal that reads, "P.S. I love you," and stuck it on my bathroom mirror where I'd have to read it at least twice a day while I cleaned my teeth. At first, I cringed each time I saw it. But now it makes me smile, and persist. Not one person who's visited my home has ever come out of the bathroom and called me a narcissist!

A mirror practice like this can be a powerful tool to shift your perspective, even if it just makes you laugh at yourself once in a while. And if the thought of it makes you squirm, perhaps try asking yourself that big question…

"What am I afraid of?"

---

1. "Fear: What Happens in the Brain and Body?" Www.medicalnewstoday.com, www.medicalnewstoday.com/articles/323492#Triggering-the-response. Accessed Nov 9, 2022
2. Zelano, Christina, et al. "Nasal respiration entrains human limbic oscillations and modulates cognitive function." Journal of Neuroscience 36.49 (2016): 12448-12467.
3. Boardman, Caroline. "The Interaction of Dopamine Levels and Proper Breathing – Breath Your Way to Good Health!" Real Wellness Doc, 25 Apr. 2018, realwellnessdoc.com/2018/04/25/the-interaction-of-dopamine-levels-and-proper-breathing-breath-your-way-to-good-health/. Accessed 9 Nov. 2022.
4. Harper, Kelly L., Kari M. Eddington, and Paul J. Silvia. "Perfectionism and effort-related cardiac activity: Do perfectionists try harder?." PloS One 11.8 (2016): e0160340.

The End

What to do next...

Leonardo da Vinci is credited as saying a work of art is never finished, there just comes a point at which the artist abandons it. He was an ingeniously creative man and is still considered one of the greatest painters in the entire history of art, despite the fact he died more than 500 years ago. If that was his benchmark, it's good enough for me.

As I mentioned in the preface, this is a short book. I wanted to leave you with an understanding about the physiological root of perfectionism, and some useful tools to take into your daily practice. Even the simple ideas in this book will make a big difference to your life, your health and your happiness.

On the next page, I've suggested a couple of more substantial books to get you started. If you want to know more about the power of the breath, give them a try.

But most of all, remember this: you are a wonderful work in progress. And with any luck, you will be for the rest of your wonderful life!

Further reading

- *Breath: The New Science of a Lost Art*, by James Nestor (2020)
- *The Breathing Cure: Exercises to Develop New Breathing Habits for a Healthier, Happier and Longer Life*, by Patrick McKeown (2021)

You can purchase The Breathing Cure or the specialist lip tape MyoTape using the QR codes overleaf.

MyoTape is a brilliant product, developed by Patrick McKeown from his 20-plus years of clinical experience. And I use *The Breathing Cure* when I'm working with clients. It's full of useful, relevant information and easy-to-follow breathing exercises.

These are affiliate links from Oxygen Advantage® and I will earn a commission on your purchase.

The Breathing Cure

MyoTape

About the Author

I'm a writer, violinist, visual artist and Oxygen Advantage® breathing instructor. I write about all things health and wellness, because I enjoy communicating information that helps people do better and feel better.

If you'd like to connect with me, you'll find me on LinkedIn at www.linkedin.com/in/johanna-mcweeney-health-and-wellness-copywriter/

And if it's your thing, you're welcome to check out my paintings at johannamcweeney.com

Printed in Great Britain
by Amazon